I0626399

Joseph Noble

Listening Voices

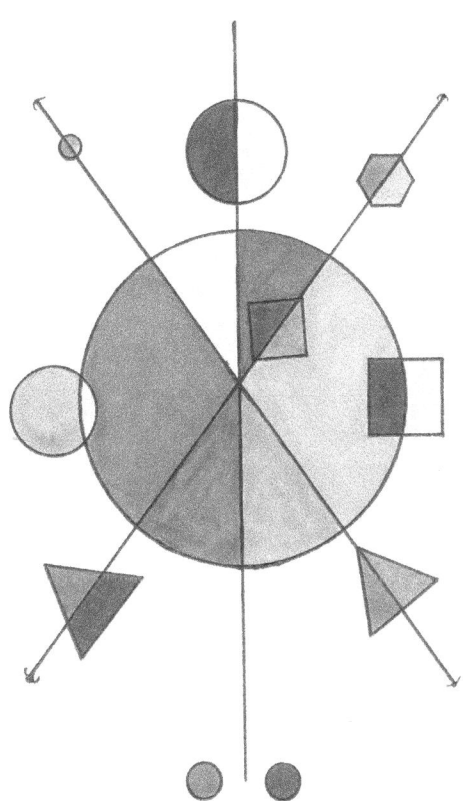

Wet Cement Press

Acknowledgments:

Eight poems from Carroway Seeds appeared in *Bird Dog*, Issue Four, Summer 2003: "3a," "3b," "3c," "3d," "3e," "41a," "41b," "41c"
Two poems from Songs and Definitions appeared in *Parentheses*, Issue 5, 2022: "song" (here is hearing) and "definition" (nothing but eyes and hands)
Five poems from Listening Voices appeared in *CSPS Poetry Letter*, No.2, June 2025: "Tone's Bones," "Diorama," "Descent," "Itself Fugue," "Toccata"

Cover artwork, "Rhythm Wheel" by Joseph Noble

Wet Cement Press
1908 Yolo Ave
Berkeley, CA 94707

www.wetcementpress.com

Contents

Carroway Seeds

Boogie Woogie Suite

3a

boogie reach
teaches bent interval
how to devil may care

sped hole hammers
crowd toward
each musical anvil

mechanical skin
takes place at
levered beats

boogie man
hammers apertures
releasing breath

3b

what is it say
doesn't have to say
is hear say

street slang
slung hand over
hand out

rhythm is
its own
hungry bone

3c

say such

      almost as if

      all most a shift

stride

      performing a place

      through the hands

3d

```
laconic
    tonic's
    tone led


s    s    h
t b t b t a
e y e y h n
p    p  e d


s
  l
    u
      r
        red note's
blue
e
  n
t


              r         c
        e roundabout e
              t         n
          a      n      d
            p
              o
                i
                  notgetting
                    t      o
                      e
                        d
                          l                    p.o.  in
                            y              a          t
```

3e

another step places hands
strut along keys walking tone
to tune about the feet's rag
tag time splits left-handed
compliments melody varies
line and space across sing bass
to chord untied notes stride

as such
and saunter
so

20

"ink marking where they
pushed a key down...
after that, they went back and
punched the holes by hand"

each hole
by longitude
and latitude
a tone

turns lost
in a cloud
following the
rain patter

rein pattern
in ear, in air
"whenabouts in the
name of space"

tone in time
marked on page
rain in air
beat in time

a long when
during where
an inkling
in scape

"There are holes that
let in more air
or less air"

44

hand to hand
    is word of mouth
what is asked for
    for what is asked
hand to mouth
    is word at hand

heel to toe
almost what
    carries to
to carry
    what at most is
cheek to cheek

    tongue in cheek
is what word
    carries return
into turn
    turns into
air's arc

dogs bark
    in the sun
air to air
    sweet-gum seed-
ball bounced
    hand to hand

41a

on time

telling told

                                                the room waiting

what's coming to

                                              allows what had been allowed

the time in the attic

                                      the room no longer a room

at the window's lip

                                   existing to be inhabited

or in the cellar

                            greater than the sum of its space

                     "living in this house that is gone"

in the earth's ear

         the body's memory

the body moves

inhabits a time

through a time

in its skin

        repeated in space

writes through

               a room day-dreamed actual

the room

             the first room

its encounter with which

               built from subsequent rooms

takes place at the tongue

                 originating from what

orienting us continually

              it will be

in a space quickened

                 each next moment

to elapse at rest

41b

o   'n

on   each

one   sound

drop   measures

by drop   its existence

words almost   by duration in

at will arise as we   the ear defining next

revolve around each other
                                                to and that between being

in the very nature of what
                                                a bit of air in a bit of time

we are distinctions of
                                                a to to a fro that's a way

sound and silence
                                                at come around gait's

accustomed to   gate dwelling in

ourselves add   telling apart

to 'n fro   listen in

to a   one by

t   one

41c

the room waiting
quickens to elapse at rest
each time allows what had been allowed
to and fro
a room by duration
greater than the sum of its words
a room no longer a room measures what's coming to

the ear defines the body's memory
a bit of air in a bit of time
taking place at will arises
we are distinctions of telling told sound
listening in
inhabiting a continual tongue
a dwelling moment

4

whose walk is it

who walks

who walks toward

around and about

is toward

who walks

a measure of distance

gravel and sand

grackle's steps

crack at the beak

bowlegged cry

what sing said

ruffled still skin

said sand slipped

glass lipped passage

egg cracked time

bows finger

thumbed toward

another step

walks toward

who it is

walks

5

what is between breath   measures recollection   birches inhabit   name out of thin air   placed
born wordless   in a named place   second skin   asked of   what it is   and   what it is to be
a room   lost in the world   before we called out in it   before we called out to it
dogwood and crabapple   define the eye   at the yard's edge
who spoke, wrote   who wrote, listened   who listened, echoed   who echoed, breathed
when away   what is a way back   is speech at the ear   away back
the desk returns to the hands   bidden and bidding   exchange   place for a place
our breath   dwelling within walls   not yet built   against which we lean
in the wall mirror   we see our breath   and behind that   our faces
the room became a word   before you   what is asked for   in what is answered
your breath fills the space   that defines where you dwell   that which leaves you   is what you enter
spun telling   on which singing hangs   by a breath

6

moving through the house   a "daydream of elsewhere"   dwelled upon   on the train
        the house moving at the doorknob   turns upon the hand   dwelling within the approach

moving through the landscape   inviting reflection   ranging through homes   thought within
        the passage   to the body's steps   invites entry   to the house

at a glance   to glance at another   one's own found   in found thought
        dwelling in the body   that sets the table   washes the glasses   built by the moment's wrist

ranging through glances   dwelled upon   elsewhere   where you sit
        the hand approaching   origin's action   building the chair anew   through skin touching wood

in rhythms   arriving and departing   the chair made   enters our rhythm
                housed in breath
        the eye's glance   turns to a gaze   and the table   enters our touch

14

how does what
we come upon
come to be
what dwells with us?
how do we learn
to live with
what we gather
that dwells
within our living
within themselves?

"I
am
my
own
hiding
place."

22

around the corner
down the hall
behind the door
within the chair
the book's skin
held in the hands
between the leaves
word to word
peered beyond
to see yourself
reading within
the space you wrap
around the corner
you turn and
nestle within

within that place
not spoken
where you dwell
you rest
a return you are
always dreaming
and moving through
from which you see
beyond the leaves
or around the corner
the place you
move into
trembling space
hand to skin
word to air

air nestles
upon earth's
turned up lips
a song invisible
within the leaves
coaxes our return
we swallow
the leaf from the nest
of the unseen bird
and doggedly sniff out
the tune we hum
a threshold turned upon
to move towards
measure's pleasure
we inhabit

26

          in the chamber

a body   a sound

          spirals

around   itself

          slowly

from out   side in

          side step

approaches   its form

          slowly

head   foot

          circles itself

mantle speaks   a house

          from the lip

hole   tone

          inhabited muscle

entered   through

          spun shell

dwelled   telling

the way in   through   the way out

Tango?

hovering dragonflies
change levels

pairs of wing pairs
echo sediment's glint

sandstone
crumbles apart

into parts of
stone sand

shale lines
crisscross

bird songs and
pine whispers

mirror
across winds

strung apart
strummed together

35 landscape with lizard

earth
  and water
                                                                          bit of
                                                                  bark leapt off
    within its scales   soil   the trunk
    bark burrows air   twitches up
          a cinder toe
          scaly, dry
to where it dwells   spinning green   tiny, brown
            outgrowth: poised wrinkle

                                    branch burr   skull
                                                    swivels then
                        invisible stillness   gone

37

thin fingered leaves
holding white
five-pointed star
    flower from
    Leander's hand
    deadly poison or
      curative broth
      ever green blooming
      in dry rock
        white whorl
        flower wheel
        with five vanes
        points in the
        direction of
        the wind's lips
        quivering in
        silent reed

to mute reel
rills sea spray
in still flight

fluted quill
over the deck
gull hovers

passed by the boat
in the unmarked sea
bird floats

toward itself
drawing the eye
black speck

flock found light
  the sound behind
each bird's eye

rides ear drum
  toward the next
wing wave

syrinx arc
  tympan wing
cleave air with

seen notes
  from feather
and throat

floating in
  parallel motion
lens humming

you find   place sounding   bird ring   bell day   standing still
     on the corner   or stepping from   one place to another   written through   cricket pulse
rhythm light   sidewalk reel   wind breath   scores stone   clef cleaves cleft
     air within air   seeing heard   map dance   dwelling light   tone steps
from lips   spinning legs   approaching where   finding place   through voice

                                                                song in the street
                                                            heard source unseen   sidewalk's gesture
                                    is felt here   parable's parabola   followed to   listening along
                   to the horizon   hic et nunc   tongue vibrating   the sparrow's gaze   its line of sight
eyes flattening   what is scarcely   lived through   at an angle equal to   motionless   hearing the direction   of silence
                        being there   elsewhere   the direction in which   for an instant
                                        in the ear   we are listening

"I take off the little chalice

"I was just going to call you.

" —TRYING OUT A PARALLEL WAY OF LISTENING TO MUSIC,

by means of the web

I've been straightening myself out

"...WITH HAYDEN FULL DAYLIGHT POURS IN

SUGGESTED BY LOOKING AT A VIEW WITH THE EYES

of long silk threads that covers it...

now that I'm back home.

FROM OUTSIDE, FROM NATURE, FROM HIS HOME

TOWARD THE SKY OR TOPS OF THE TREES,

The lower lip of the flower

I've been away.

FROM PLACES WHICH FOR A ROBUST AND NATURAL MAN

TAKING IN THE EARTH OR FOREGROUND SUBJECTIVELY—

is straight and a bit folded under;

I don't know where.

FORM THE TRUE BASIS OF HIS IMAGINATION AND HIS LIFE

THAT IS, NOT FOCUSING THE EYE ON IT—

it is a deep pink on the inside,

No?

THEN LOOKING AT THE EARTH AND LAND,

and on the outside is covered with thick fur.

Well, it's felt like I've been away."

The entire plant causes smarting when touched.

AND SEEING THE SKY

"The dogwood leaves are turning red,

"I hate it when I can't remember.

It wears a typically northern costume

AND THE TOP OF THE FOREGROUND SUBJECTIVELY.

and the sunlight twinkles among them.

I get so mad at myself. It's my fault.

with four little stamens

IN OTHER WORDS,

The asters bear white blooms that shine

Why can't I remember?

that are like little yellow brushes."

GIVING A MUSICAL PIECE

like snow under the blue sky.

I ask myself, 'Where was I?'

IN TWO PARTS,

And a little bush is loaded with ruby red berries.

I got out of their car and couldn't remember

BUT PLAYED

I tasted a berry, and it tasted bad."

where I'd been. Maybe being back

AT THE SAME TIME—

in my place made me forget."

inscrutable wind
scripts grass tempo
feathers level corn
past the ear
tassels shake wings
flat to weather
determined
rubber and metal
pass over
inhabited blacktop
inscribed wind
threads air
through rock to pull
water stopped at a
moth on the melody

soil syrinx

coils throat

larynx stem

tests the field

swaying root wind

spins around grass

from inside out

and about

within the great plain
the car moves
within the eye
black seed
rooted on either side
of the hole
that is itself
passage making
things real
storm in one corner
sun in another
in space we move
through the eye
to change places
with ourselves

shore

enough to confound

passage

through time and again

at least both

left with

one sand

sure

what's it
  why isn't it   a woman walking
    here I can
     that's it
a maple   *move a little*
      there past
    oh, man!   weeds through sidewalk cracks
   what's he
braking for   clouds between buildings
   now if
    I can just
     yea, that's it   a dog sniffing a hydrant
      good
a couple having dinner *now make*
       this light
   sparrows fly up   *then the turn*
      what's   someone whistling
two men talking   *what's this one*
     waiting for   newspapers
  streetlights   *come on*
    it's just   the wind blowing leaves
   a few blocks
   you'd think a boy on a bike
  I were
  asking for   stars
the world

                    the acorn
                     splits
                   into itself
                opening its mouth
                   to become
                  many tongues
                     split
                   into each
                    instant
                 filling the sky
sparrows   wrens
        warblers   robins
                    mockingbirds   chickadees
                      towhees   thrushes
                         finches
fly through their song   seeds between their beaks

                  twittering nests

                     the call
                comes across
                   the field
                 hanging where
                   it moves
                slowly gathering
                 to it the place
                 to which it
                gathers itself
                  as it moves
                   through

                 hearing's reach
              within breathing room

Afterword

Two prime sources of inspiration for *Carroway Seeds* are Conlon Nancarrow's *Studies for Player Piano* and Gaston Bachelard's *A Poetics of Space*. Heidegger's thoughts on dwelling also find their way somewhat into the poems. In addition, I am grateful to Kyle Gann for his book, *The Music of Conlon Nancarrow*, as well as to Charles Amirkhanian for his work in bringing Nancarrow's music to a wider audience.

One of the main concerns of the series is space, both in what the poems talk about and in how they appear on the page. Many aspects of space figure in the content of the poems: dwelling in space; moving through it; people and things in relation to each other in space and to the space itself; the relation between time, space, living, and memory. In these poems, space is where being takes place, where meaning happens.

The form that each poem takes is from the Nancarrow study whose number precedes it. I tried to create visual and verbal correlatives to the Nancarrow pieces, which are used as jumping off points. Yet, each poem in the series can stand on its own without reference to the Nancarrow study. So, as with the poems in my book, *An Ives Set,* a dialogue between interdependence and independence takes place in this series too.

Also, because of the way a few of the poems appear on the page, each of these particular poems can be read as containing several poems within it. In these poems, all stanzas function together as one poem, yet each stanza functions also as a separate poem, and, in addition, all the lines in the whole poem can be read in varying order, thereby again creating multiple poems. In addition, poem No. 37 contains 12 poems (or poems within poems) that can be read together or separately.

So a dichotomy between connection and autonomy exists in the series both in the poems' connections to and autonomy from the Nancarrow study to which each poem refers, as well as within each particular poem itself in how the stanzas relate to each other, and in the series as a whole in how each poem is both independent from and connected to the series itself.

Songs and Definitions

definition

around the voice
is its own call
careful air with reach
cell by cell, glass by grass
curious with beat
song aligns and allows
mind's difference and grace
wood and limestone
build notes with corners
there are keys and there are hairs
what splits is air
voice is name and touch
the tongue sings what is something else

song

here is hearing
of one voice
listening

the spoken word
is now sung speech

echo aria
of its own
sounding first

part poem
part song

each voice
descant
upon the other

definition

nothing but eyes and hands
pigeons are wood
dovetailing stickball
with lovemaking
breath articulates the sky
rounds the corner with grass
before one can summon up
where to walk to
an ear appears
signing the tune
it hears
street wing is wind
swallows and syllables

definition and song

bones in the sky
covered with leaves and wires
a song playing about them

stone is kilowatt and finger
shake sake and sound
who is why that walks

paper scape
shutter split
bedspring blink

skid loud and sardine

definition

within the tree
there is a bone that sings

spin sill and wire time
hand flat at tock

to and fro whistle
on the stairs

these feet do not realize
they do not want
the footprints they do not have

sing and sign
interlope along

what is expected to last
vanishes
what is expected to vanish
sustains

song

a word not said
was sung
and though
he was not there
to hear it
the silence
he listened to
was given voice
by what
he did not hear

song

the lips open
upon a breath
they make possible
and given to them
by a rhythm
of the song sung
along the way

definition and song

frame and finesse
arcs moving through angles

body brings flesh through streets
movement among edifices

garden voice rummaging among
fruit and bones

the ground is tender
sparkling with buttons

In the Air

fingering
each note
flesh and bone
alight upon what
is carried through

a conversation
measures passing
with the breath
figuring the movement
of the air

composed with two
pairs of lips
and that which
is both
and neither

rises to be
yet is of
an opening held
at the moment
the breath moves

iron tuned
fountain joint

moment between
the fingers

mirror tone
frailing light

twin dust
another compass

sun's ladder
a rung bone
in the sky

humming against
the ramparts
holding up ilium

bluebird flies
from the hipbone
aster in mid-air

the tree holds
a single apple
a single coral

light grows
a wing
in the hipbone

spicules splinter
in the dust wondering
what to become

blink flint
falls through
candle spoke

print on eyelid
creates the sky

names in the
alphabet's wick
light-shock's letter

print on sky
creates the eyelid

a finch glides
through the map

tight wire aria
tripwire arm

glass in the kitchen
light unknowing

choral delight
beside each noon

slip canto
strung echo

wooden bread
dreams a corner
filled with holes

tense smoke
brick at falling
mortared sky
crumbled
shell to word
bird through
the space
no longer
occupied

gnat scribbling
on white paper

tiny eyed silence
moving

spoor letter
contending knuckle's argot

the hand
inherits the instant

the sun hard in your face
you count its fingers

dust's syrinx
rattles air

redoubtable
recounting

your mouth
another mute mechanism

blinker stem
ore cortex

augury naming silence

intoned silence
dust hum

horizon exiled
by being seen

breath appears
in the compass needle

keening ears
mute abandon

sere grieving
plays the bone

corner tone's
cloud rope

told to light
pulse marrow

speech tendon's
reed trace

silence begins to hum
air takes shape

south sings with dust

an appearance is recorded
in the voice's tones

north tunes a stone

breath builds speech's horizon
melody its compass needle

west turns a corner

an unheard tune is followed:
silence played through the bone

east hums with footsteps

the note is not round
it is not perfect and centered in itself
it is not part of a melody
nor does it contribute to any harmony
it creates no pitch
it makes no sound
it is nothing you would expect
and nothing you would not expect
it cannot be articulated by the fingers or tongue
words cannot describe it nor call it forth

you have played the note
as if it were not played

Listening Voices

for Ray Ernst
in memoriam

Inventions

s(ay)ing

as(you would)say

each(through)note

      Speech
      Turns
      Refines
      In
      Note's
      Grace

your accept/dancing

throug)hand(through

a s(you say)ing

to y(our)ears

stringtheory

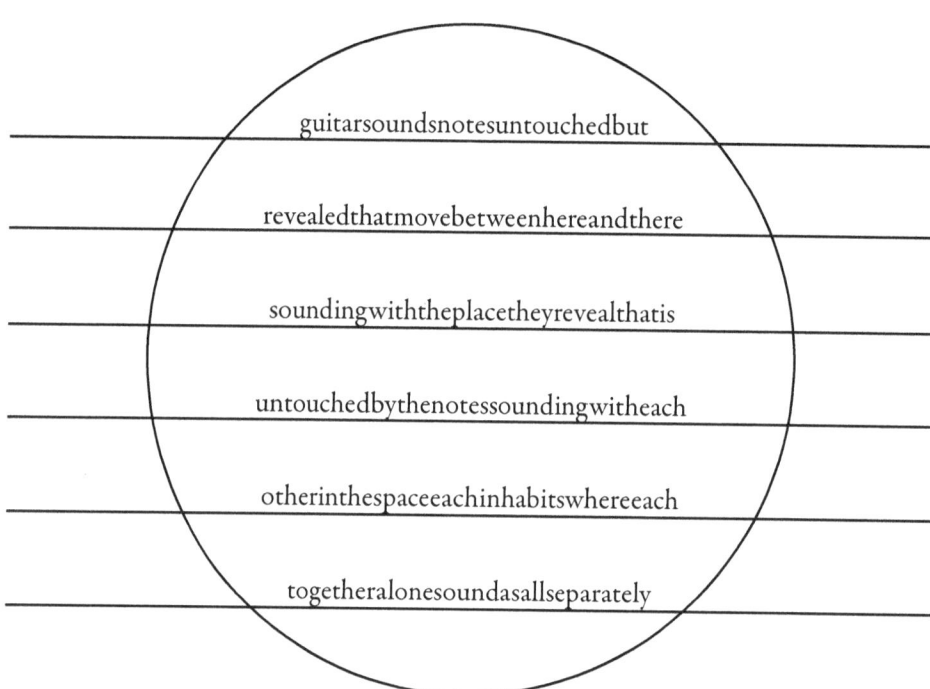

guitarsoundsnotesuntouchedbut

revealedthatmovebetweenhereandthere

soundingwiththeplacetheyrevealthatis

untouchedbythenotessoundingwitheach

otherinthespaceeachinhabitswhereeach

togetheralonesoundasallseparately

circular breathing

passage passing through thought appears in ears is sound

strum rung strung time sprung rhythm rhyming light

lingual touch ringing tells bell's tongue tolling sung

note as it is silenced is heard

echo mirror

you disappear in the notes   notes vanish in the mirror
I speak your name   name the hearing
lips voice a shadow   shadow voices a breath
you appear   a peering echo
shadow the tune   tune the shadow
found in hands   hand's foundling
in wind's words   words unwind
spire light   lyre sight

tone's bones

tone angling
through bone
shadow hearing
itself
tendon string
ringing wood
and air
body a mystery
with blood
forgetting its
own pitch
and place
humming
the memory
becoming
the note
on the lips
weightless in
its trilling
spilling within
its echo
a disappearance
manifesting itself
before the ears

rays up

r	r
a	a
y	e
f	p
a	p
l	a
l	o
s	t
t	d
o	n
a	a
s	g
o	n
u	i
n	s
d	o
t	t
o	p
a	u
s	s
i	e
g	s
h	i
t	r

as met

mirror speaks to its own voice
r
      one light as it is heard in another
u
n
  sounding in the eyes
t
h
e
  key and string turn in the touch
o
t
fingers ring tones from silver and wood
s
a
s
unseen and untouched
h
e
y
s
though plucked or tongued
u
n
d
  song as it is met
i
l
the pupil the sound hole
n
t
the eyelid the ear shell
y

upon silence

upon

    song

listening

          outward

    continuously   silence

string

          expands

    climbs   finds

rings

          inward

    backward   missing

point

          lengthens

    descends   note

to

          shortens

    forward   playing

point

          sounds

    contracts   unheard

          silences

             silence

unison's intervals

(incog~sub terra~nita)

un)heard(sounding

(t)f(h)i(r)n(o)g(u)e(g)r(h)
grass

hand's
t|a|b|l|a|t|u|r|e

p.l.u.c.k. and s-t-r-u-m

with(beat and beats)in

~f~r~e~q~u~e~n~c~i~e~s'~
frequencies

be
l in l
the
grass
  i i
  n n
  g g
  i i
  n n
  g g

Fugues

Light Fugue

the light as is
is not a sound
yet as it is
is a sound that
quivers into view

the light falls
upon the hands
that strum the strings
strung across
the still silence

you as you were
are in our eyes
seeming to be
as you were
seen to be

though you
are no longer
a breath
or sound
before us

though we
hear your voice
and hear your song
that quivers your
image into view

the light
as it is sung
is a light of
a different hue
a light only heard

Silent Fugue

you walk into the mirror,
    in your hands the notes
        unimagined and unthought

unarticulated and unheard—
    a shadow, you pull ghost notes from the guitar
        for us to hear in all their absence—

the guitar is itself a shadow
    newly formed each moment
        a shadow body waiting to be touched—

the songs you had not yet
    imagined are singing,
        springing from your shadow fingers

and the shadow guitar
    a twining from wound strings
        and tendon's twine

a twinning between the two
    turning and tuning both air and breath
        in a shadow tune

as we listen in the silence
    to the silence that is there
        and the silence that is not

Enharmonic Fugue

You knew each string as it defined itself:
sounded ore twisted into wound cords,
quivering from your hands that wound chords
through the split air, a wound corded with fingers,

enharmonic with its own healing.
You knew each sound and its chosen light:
the finch moved between its notes and
was its own twin disappearing in its song,

note upon the dark, an amulet for the voice.
Sound we could not hear but listened to,
sound that was silent as your hand
that made a sound beyond itself.

This was the sound you wrote upon
your body: a tattoo's tell, a scar's scoring.
What you could not hear you felt in the wound's
scribblings: a braille unspoken by the hands.

We heard it in our voices, in the finch feather's flutter,
We heard it and did not know why we heard it,
though we looked for it without searching for it:
a light ringing in the hands,

a song we heard lost in the air
an air we heard in the song we lost,
ear to ear, a sound of sounds still
resounding, as if we never heard them.

Shadow Fugue

what the sound meant
turning in the recognition

ray in the doorway
humming with notes

name at the threshold
burning with silence

tones plucked but untouched
appearing unseen

each together alone
sounding as all separately

we listen and hear silently
sound as turning string

sound steel quivering
into sight unseen

the hand as it plays
upon touch dreaming

breath with what air
mute in speaking what song

your ears listening for
question and answer

voice upon voice that
only your fingers apprehend

in your hand the little snail's
antennae are ringing sunward

their sand threading
through your tongue

a moment revolving in the tree
gone again from your lungs

chanting with arched back
you step between intervals

plucking unheard notes
your shadow touches

Double Fugue

You had thought of the sound,
and it was coming to meet you;

it was declaring itself as it sounded.
What it was and what it did

were one and the same as it met you
climbing the stairs or walking the dog.

It was the sound you thought of
before you sounded it, before it sounded.

But if you sounded it, had it no life of its own;
was the sound only of you and by you and from you?

The sound rounded out itself; it spoke its sound;
it circled the dog or sat on the stairs

waiting for a pair of ears to hear it; it nestled
next to you as you sat on the sofa and thought of it.

Who was to know its tone; who was
to sound the depths of what was sounding?

As soon as you sounded it, it was there.
Though it came from you, or at least of your

creation, it was not you, but was itself
as it is itself, heard in its own mirror,

a doubling identity of one in and of itself
as itself in contemplation of what it is,

neither sound nor the making of sound but
rather sound coexistent with itself as is and as it is.

But still, you made the sound, you plucked the string,
and you listened to the sound as you played, as it sounded;

you listened to yourself sounding the sound,
to yourself sounding, your ears resounding

with the sound you had plucked from silence
that gave back, that gave itself in response,

the little snail alive with it, you alive with it,
resounding as the one sounding and sounded.

Itself Fugue

you as you neither came to be
        nor as you would come to be
                but as you are continually coming to be—

when your song ended
        it was not the end of your song
                but an echo remained

a reminder remanded
        to nowhere but elsewhere
                a sounding in itself—

the cricket strides its stridulation
        out into plain hearing
                to woo or to warn

but the song of its song
        doesn't care for its intent
                intending to be nothing

other than it is
        a song for the hearing
                a song without an echo

that is an echo itself
        that the cricket plays
                upon its wings

and listens to
      as it plays:
            both song and singer

sound and echo
      here and nowhere
            now and when

Tone Rows

1

sparrow scales spill
nimble rill
stone shard sparks tone
grass blade's bone

lark reels, plumbs
pass a mezzo syrinx bone
reed ore hums auricle

finch peals rose ring
pocketful of breath poses
ash tongue's mute hum

cicada trills lizard's
languid etude
—wink and hunger—
fish scale sky

2

riddle dawn, blue geyser
glowworm shadow, lantern hand
sky forest chants eyelids

noon stone, desert weave
madrigal bell calls water
sand mirrors guitar light

dusk rivulet pours swallows
swarming grove flute's
shadow wet leaves'
cricket sleeves

hunger, tune, hand
—whisper to the air—
run ahead to hear yourself

3

they do not know
who they are invoking
by plucking each string

dust in the wind
makes a sound
as it rubs against nothing

sounds plucked from the stream:
whole or half steps
never the same

hand as not
—shadow strum—
hand as thought
here as ear hears

4

crow crinkle quarter note
clinks agate
river rides with
horn bearing sea

turning light
in its sound
fingers listen
geode pitched
an octave below

photo shiver
ducks into clothes
time rambles on about
moonstone borrowing rhythm

pebble path traversed through
listening familiarly foreign
—hungry, you swallow the note—

5

skin sight?
redemption or resurrection?
the hand still queries
the other question

voice elapsed, plucked,
the distance interrupts
by coming closer

thin silver lightning's still second
fingers the flute
trinkle tinkle tones twinkle

—witness your absence—
your skin having become
its own twin sound

6

lantana umbel umbrel's
tentacle stems
dangle in tidal air
wet with wind

flutter tongue fins
its way through
flute's reed heart
hollow with tones

whole stone's fish scales
step by step iridescent
waver neither and either

water dreams song's
reed mist
—step through tones, wet—
sand slipped fingers

7

absence again, the word
an emotion only satisfied
by the word grief

the stories only
we knew
I speak now
only to the breath

your hand silent
the string unplucked
yet stretched between us
thrumming mutely

—vulnerable as living without—
you are found without
within what's not found

Songs

In the Ligature

the feather sings wind's finch
the apteryx's cicatrix grows wings

weather discovers itself in its own ringing
the hand claps with its own shadow

the notes ride logic, word for word
bottlebrush branch tits burgeon budding beaks

it is in your hand that the relinquished voice
enables you to find the ability to sing

summer is its own weightless remembrance
the boat in the park, hovering on the mirror

where did you find the capricious sorrow
the fingers of the chord lingering in the vine

Amulet

fountain and finch beforehand
leaf calling another wing

riding light its own granite
hunger as it befalls itself

we ghost, we sound ear to ear
wheel and weather tuning feather

this hand is strung with ore and fire
and air is a revelation for remembering

sting tune reels the fingers
sun amulet rubbed in the pocket

Diorama

the bus had its own levitation device
each tone initiating a harbinger feather

a weathered voice discoursed upon
tiny bodies filled with perpetual sand

the museum's diorama hopped on one leg
an explorer whistling for home

the tibia was the aulos in the body
the fingers the five string lyre

what domain were we invoking
in our lexical wheelhouse?

we found the mirror on the store rack
an image of breath for the ears

Hunger Tongue

the sound is what made us visible
octaves tight around the corners
we walked through each note
with our hands intact

count on the silence
to make its own tone row
the notes growing skins
we could feel between our fingers

each ear had its own belly to feed
the blessed one counting his bones
through which he blew a tune
chewing on its own audibility

Auricle

grass whispers as it burns
weed reed a tablature for breath
tones through eyes touch ash

the mirror dances with its own echo
from which you pluck another hand that is
your own, born as you open your lips

the shadow opens its mouth and releases its shadow
the pendulums continue counting backwards
the ribs are stolen from the wheelwright's pulse

the shadow holds its echo, turns it in its hand
looking for its soul, listening for a sound deep in its
occlusion, a crescent shadow thrown upon itself

auricle is the passageway through which you travel
an elsewhere neither nowhere nor somewhere—
neither absence nor presence, you are known through hearing

Who

who as you as
an other another

listening and hearing
an echo sounded

before the sound
sang into view

Descent

you are breathing where you no longer stand
light coexistent with the sound it makes
a quivering where you had seen the music

the song has walked down into the shadows
that listen to its mute lips
its hands on the corners of sound, waiting

you follow her with your ears
that guide you through the dark
through the silence breathing your listening

when you open your lips, there's silence
and closing them, you hear the song
singing mutely in its plenitude

Dialogue

you have always been this way
you have never been this way

your voice has receded into
what you did not say

you are speaking to yourself
in a language you don't understand

letters form on your tongue
that you do not recognize

they do not spell out your voice
only what you did not leave behind

in the story, the song is
plucked from your hand

your lungs disappear
in the unplayed sonata

your voice's archive appears
in its own lapse in memory

the guitar carries
a song it gives you

touching your hand that
gives a song to its strings

Telling

the thought as it would have been thought—yours—
what you brought to the surface, what you dislodged—

the shadows we saw did not speak
yet we heard them through how we saw them
they stood among the silence as it echoed—

your hand vanishing touched the sound—
your shattered body that you left in the silence
had its own pitch and timbre—

this is the body we wake in each morning
telling us of nothing other than its breath and rhythm
the corporeal incorporeality shivering in the flesh
welling up through the throat and birthing from the lips

Toccatas

the breath had carried itself out into the air
where it realized it was speaking

if you had any light, it was
this one with its back to the wall

another quarter note, and you could create
a language each transposition could suggest

pressing the flesh with the guidonian hand
the fingers were sticky with pitch

earth bell ringing with distance
string ore talking with tree roots

what was the shadow's last name
humming between the sheets

awake in the echo, seamless to the night
a whistle relinquished to its better half

isorhythmic light in the voice's color
tenor slips word and tone through echo's answer

weaving chant as invitation, a heat spell in the antiphony
eye music's word painting at the back of its own neck

a dance as contrary motion intoning the body
limbs figuring the moment's notation

the mirror's inversion is played by its echo
in retrograde, pitched to movable do's silence

strings becoming tendons becoming shadows
how many fingers am I holding up?

as you were saying to yourself
as you were saying to me

the tune was following its own tail
seminarians nudging the offbeat

you spoke with the angel about
his lack of diminished chords

you augmented your studies with
little rootie-tootie's kitchen modes

you meditate in high-monkery
the notes levitating in your breath

say it as sung, say it as heard to be
listening states its own appearance

the soundboard split from the tree
and entered the radio's field of vision

each chord was an instant, an instance
where the guitar found its own fingers

you were broken in the sound
the strings torn from each limb

but the trees and buildings were silent
your cries having entered their shadows

said spoke shine spins singing
string light strung scordatura

standing where you no longer stood, you remembered
your silence, humming just out of earshot

relinquishing as finally finding hands
glissando signed sand in cursive

if you wondered, you plucked ink
waiting couldn't be any more crystalline

whistle the threadbare wanting for question
hazard chimes in the memory pain

breath note was carrying the off beat
picture tube spinning bridge and refrain

bare knees waiting for known, for moon heckler
we had found high monkery in background music

playing behind your back came forward
into the tremor fret's beeline miles

you tempered the touch
each as what was coming to speak

as what was heard in the silent room
the steps moving obliquely with the key in the door

this listening, as it stared
this transposition in the reflection and echo

where found, your voice in the skin tunes its filament
your body in migration around your retina

you are neither singing nor not singing
time tuning itself through another's tongue

you are neither here nor not here
neither playing inside nor outside the changes

breath is the hand between
the leaf as it has not stated itself

breath walks between itself
waiting already past to come

breath doesn't exist
but keeps talking to itself

breath forgot who
it was playing a duet with

breath listens to the flute
and waits for its entrance

breath sings a lot
when it listens to its voice

you as you were
saying as sing as hand light

shimmer tone ringing touch
speaking no harm for what not said

and singing care for what said
as was for now in the hearing

you came and stood as sound
speaking as knowing as listening

as playing as singing as sounding
as greeting as leaving as being

you as you were as you are
tone touching tongue and finger

ray rung riddle's pitch print
switches sung light note to note—

sounding mote sings sight,
writ tongue wrangling water hum—

strings flex steel wrung tones,
reel sprung—wick wheel kindle to cloud

blinks aloud—bone light limbs
flint the sound spindle—

on mica glint streets, prism hymn
walks beat, concrete heat squints

pica flight through the mirror,
wing image sleight of echo

Fantasias

We found ourselves at night in the midst of shadows. On the unfamiliar road, plants took the form of mute voices. We saw trees still and quiet. We stood motionless, watching their silence, finding each note from our hands between their leaves.

Breath a letter awaiting inscription. Note skimming wall and corner. Air as it was spoken. Limbs in translation. Palms glistening with melody. Apples invoking daylight. Rain savors the equidistant wind. Light whistles through the sun, a marsh bird on its shoulder.

We found our hands immersed in the most curious music. We turned round to witness the sound's breathing. Wood, air, string. The port had moved its destination. Floaters flew with birds, discovering the distance. Sparrows whispered the sky. We tried to remember what we hadn't experienced yet. The boat an eyelid on the water.

Hunger at the mirror image shoulders changeling smoke. Clay's imagination builds tendrils in the coral rites. Hum shivers. Rays ripple through hawksbill and leatherback. Eyefall the solar hand shuddering with stamens. Absent glance imperceptible in the scent. Flourishing drum running guesswork.

Where had we found the images, the mirror? In each note, the guiding hand listened to its movement. We rose from the subway, carrying water with words. Notes were dripping with altitude, soil thinking through its own alphabet. We wandered through our own gamuts, counterpoint diagrammed unrecognizably. Tablature arose from touch, tones speaking in tongues.

From sounds, we wove our hands so they were invisible to speech. We listened to footsteps that described each moment. Together, we had come upon the air without realizing it. Another breath and each tone that found its way into our skin rested there for us to discover.

Branch upon branch, maple cathedral its own garland. Acrobat notes in the sparrow throat. Bicycle stream a song for whisper birch. Street steam hot with waiting, anchoring horn to whistle heat. Searching the born melody, we touched sound with our fingers, rhododendrons blossoming within earshot in the woods.

When we were heard, we were seen. Story on a string. Pluck and pulse. Tongue taps breath on the shoulder. Tone roads lead elsewhere to be heard here. Whittled bough's wound whistle rings bark's splintered tone splits lips toward leaf's pinna listening. Sing particle pitch. Say singing echo beforehand touching listen through to sounding now in then to be. Sing speaking voice gone into the dark, into the light, into the sound. Hear and appear.

Afterword

Listening Voices is haunted by two presences. One is my friend, Ray Ernst, who died on June 14, 2023. Ray was an accomplished guitarist, multi-instrumentalist, composer, and teacher who lived and breathed music. He graduated summa cum laude in composition from Berklee School of Music—not a small accomplishment—and lived his life performing jazz, rock, nuevo flamenco, classical, and many other types of music and teaching countless students. He was my oldest and one of my dearest friends.

Ray was only one day older than me, and we met the first day of high school, having turned 14 only a month before, and became close and dear friends for the rest of Ray's life. Music was an important facet of both our lives. Having met at such an early and crucial age, we shared many important experiences and transitions together, learning much about both life and music. These experiences and what we learned became important bonds between us.

This series of poems grew out of my grief at Ray's death, which came much too soon for a person who was such a strong presence and so full of life and music. But the poems also grew out of my love for Ray and joy in our friendship, which was a relationship very singular and special in my life.

The other presence that haunts these poems is Orpheus, who has been a recurring leitmotif for me. Ray and Orpheus are intertwined in the series. The two share many aspects and mirror each other in many ways. In fact, the series can be read in at least three ways: as dealing with Ray or Orpheus or both simultaneously.

Books and works that I was reading while writing this series of poems and that have informed them include: Wallace Stevens's "The Man with the Blue Guitar" and "Notes Toward a Supreme Fiction"; Rilke's *Sonnets to Orpheus*; Dino Campana's *Canti Orfici*; and Jean-Luc Nancy's essay, "Ascoltando."

The four series in this book are part of a larger work dealing with music called *Lyra*. *An Ives Set*, the three series in *Antiphonal Air*s, and other unpublished series are also part of *Lyra*.

About the Author

Joseph Noble's poetry has appeared in *Hambone, New American Writing, Lana Turner, Seedings, Parentheses, OR,* and other journals, as well as in the anthology, *Resist Much, Obey Little*. Six poems also appeared in the San Francisco Exploratorium's exhibit, "Social Behavior Lab." He has published three books of poetry: *Within Hearing* (lyric& Press, 2018), *Antiphonal Airs* (Skylight Press, 2013), and *An Ives Set* (lyric& Press, 2006), and a chapbook, *Homage to the Gods* (Berkeley Neo-Baroque, 2012).

He received his PhD from the State University of New York at Stony Brook, where his dissertation was on the early poetry of George Oppen, three excerpts of which have appeared in *Talisman, Aufgabe, and Sagetrieb*. Another essay, "essay/assay: on sound," appeared in *Amerarcana*, No. 7.

Joseph Noble also plays flutes and saxophones in various musical groups. More information on his poetry and music can be found on his website, www.josephnoble. info.

www.ingramcontent.com/pod-product-compliance
Lightning Source LLC
Chambersburg PA
CBHW041537120626
46551CB00019B/2732